# Note for parents

The National Literacy Strategy includes a list of 45 'high frequency' words to be learnt by the end of Reception. The simple sentences in this book have been composed of these essential high frequency words to give your child the practice and confidence they need to tackle their reading.

The addition of stickers to find and place will help your child learn about numbers and counting, while becoming familiar with high frequency words in a fun way!

Start by reading this book to your child. When your child is familiar with the words and numbers, ask them to find the number and picture stickers for each page.

As your child gains in confidenc      to read the simple sentences and count by

D1341618

TOP THAT

One happy bear. He is my dad!

'I can see two little cubs,' he says.

Three big trees have green leaves.

Four buzzy bees are making honey.

Five green frogs come to sit on this brown log.

Six mummy ducks look for six of their chicks.

Seven aeroplanes fly away in the day.

# Eight fast cars ...

... driving on a number eight.

Nine butterflies can fly high up in the sky.

Ten fat cats like to sit on the mat.

Eleven dogs go to the park to play.

Twelve bugs all want leaves for lunch.

Thirteen children just like me and you.

# Fourteen cows are going to get wet!

Fifteen fairies came to tea.

They all said 'Yes!' to cake!

It was fun!

Sixteen sailing boats
sail far out at sea.

Mum has grown seventeen flowers in her garden.

'It is very pretty!' she said.

Eighteen teddy bears
that we all love.

Nineteen little monsters said ...

# Twenty toys for good girls and boys.